D0464677

Stick Together

Stick Together

*A Simple Lesson to Build
a Stronger Team*

JON GORDON   KATE LEAVELL

WILEY

Published by John Wiley & Sons, Inc., Hoboken, New Jersey.
Published simultaneously in Canada.

Illustrations by Katie Mazeika

For general information on our other products and services or for technical support, please contact our Customer Care Department within the United States at (800) 762-2974, outside the United States at (317) 572-3993 or fax (317) 572-4002.

Wiley publishes in a variety of print and electronic formats and by print-on-demand. Some material included with standard print versions of this book may not be included in e-books or in print-on-demand. If this book refers to media such as a CD or DVD that is not included in the version you purchased, you may download this material at http://booksupport.wiley.com. For more information about Wiley products, visit www.wiley.com.

Library of Congress Cataloging-in-Publication Data is Available:
ISBN 9781119762607 (Hardcover)
ISBN 9781119762652 (ePDF)
ISBN 9781119762676 (ePub)

Cover design: Paul McCarthy
Cover art: @iStock | Sun Stock

SKY113554_021121

This book is dedicated to Chris, who taught me to live life with passion, discipline, and purpose, to never give up, and to always Win the Day. Great friends Stick Together!

—Kate

To my amazing JG team who stuck together through adversity and grew stronger together.

—Jon

Contents

Chapter One

Falling Short

Coach David tossed and turned as he tried
to sleep the night before the first day of
basketball season. As a new coach last year,
with some of the best players in the state, he
was haunted by the fact that the team had
failed to live up to their potential.

He thought anxiously about how he could get his players to come together this year. He felt like he had let everyone down, because he had the best athletes and yet they weren't successful as a team. They didn't trust each other. They argued. They were negative on the court, and they didn't communicate or share the ball well.

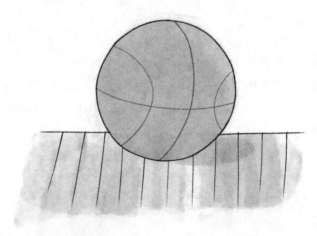

At 2 a.m. he hopped out of bed and started pacing around the kitchen. He tried drinking warm milk and snuggling with his dog Joey on the couch, but nothing helped to calm his nerves.

"OUCH!" he yelled as he jumped up from the couch. Something had poked him from under the seat cushion, so he reached down to see what it was. He pulled out a stick Joey must have buried there. It was just one of many presents Joey liked to hide around the house. He gave Joey a look of loving disapproval as he rubbed his leg.

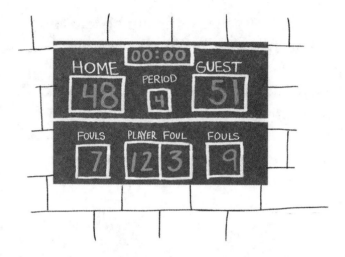

Suddenly, he remembered something his mother had told him at the end of last season when she was in town to watch their dreadful playoff game. Despite being predicted to win the championship, they lost in the first round. He was so embarrassed.

One thing she had said really stood out in his memory. She said his team reminded her of an old fable about broken sticks. He had been too disappointed at the time to listen and ask her what she meant, and he was regretting that now. His mom always had great advice, but he wasn't always the best at listening. She had passed away over the summer and he was missing her advice more than ever.

On a hunch, he jumped up and grabbed his phone for a quick internet search. He typed in "fables about sticks." He started scrolling through the results until he found it: Aesop's fable about the sticks.

This is it, he thought to himself. He looked at Joey, whose couch burying habit had sparked this idea and shouted, "JOEY, YOU'RE THE SMARTEST DOG ALIVE!" Joey, who already knew he was brilliant, yawned and snuggled in closer.

Coach David jumped up, and Joey, who was always up for an adventure no matter what time of day, jumped up and circled him, ready for action.

In the middle of the night, with Joey and his phone flashlight, Coach David crawled around his backyard woods on all fours, looking for sticks to bring to the first day of practice. Joey was happy to assist.

Excitement had taken the place of anxiety and he felt a ray of hope shining in his heart. For the first time, he felt like he had something to guide them that would be much bigger than stats, streaks, or playoffs. He had something meaningful that would give this team a stronger connection and a greater purpose.

Chapter Two

The Sticks

As the players arrived at practice the next day, Coach David stood outside the door to the locker room and handed each player a weak, skinny little stick as they walked in. On the big whiteboard, Coach had written in their team colors, "THE STICK CHALLENGE."

Each small stick had a piece of tape around one end with a word written on it. One of the players asked the coach, "Why is there a word on the stick?"

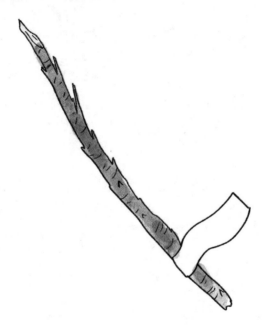

The players were laughing and comparing stick words when Coach David asked them to take a seat so he could explain. He held up a stick, just like the ones he had given the players. "Take care of your stick," he told them. "The sticks are brittle and they snap very easily. For this challenge, you don't want your stick to get broken." He snapped his stick in half, showing them how easy it was to break.

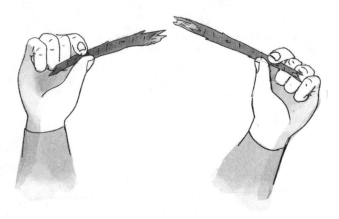

He told them the challenge had two parts. The first part, after each player got a stick with a word, was to find a partner with the same word. Together, they needed to research why a team would need that trait in order to be their best. Then they would report back to the team on their assigned day.

The second part of the challenge was that they had to make the sticks unbreakable. He then pulled out a box that was filled with the team's new uniforms. These were the uniforms they'd been hoping for, and they were printed, folded, and ready to make them look good on the court.

Coach David said, "If you figure out how to make your sticks unbreakable, you guys will be wearing THESE!" He pulled one out and held it proudly.

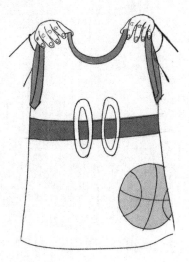

The players looked down at their thin,
brittle sticks and held them carefully.
"Coach, that's impossible!" said Isaiah.
Another team member grabbed for his stick
as a joke, and he shouted back at him, "Don't
touch it; what's the matter with you?" as he
gently put his stick in the top of his locker
and gave his teammate a little shoulder
shove. "I'm getting that uniform!"

Coach called out the first word that would be assigned for the next afternoon at practice. "The first word is Believe, and I believe that belongs to our new players this season, John and Daniel."

"New kids have to go first! Ha!" said Markell, who was a team captain from last year.

"Don't worry Markell, you're up after them on Wednesday!" said Coach David with a smile.

Markell grabbed his basketball to head out
to the court and playfully shouted back,
"I don't care, I'll do it! Can't break
MY stick!"

The next day, Markell walked into the locker room after everyone else was already sitting and ready to go. "I got this, guys!" He gave a stick to Coach that was covered in duct tape top to bottom. "It's a practice stick, I found it outside. Check it out. Unbreakable!"

Coach gave him a curious look. "Okay, let's try it out," he agreed. He took the stick between his finger and thumb in each hand. "SNAP!"

"OOOOOH!" Voices and laughter echoed through the locker room as the stick snapped right through the duct tape. "Good thing that wasn't your real stick, Markell!" said one of his teammates.

Markell sat down, "Alright, alright, it didn't work. Cheap duct tape, that's all it was."

"Okay, before we hit the court, John and Dan are up with their word. Go for it, guys," urged Coach David.

Chapter Three

Believe

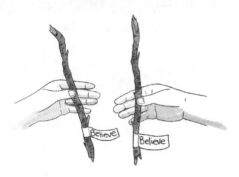

"Our word is Believe," said Dan.

"So, we looked up some reasons why a team needs to believe and what they need to believe to be successful. Teams ultimately accomplish what they collectively believe is possible and so it's important for each person on the team to believe in great outcomes and in each other. A team's collective belief must be greater than all the adversity and negativity they face. It only takes one person who doesn't believe to hurt a team. That's why a team must believe in each other, especially when a teammate is struggling with confidence and doubt."

"When team members believe in each other, that helps them fill each other up with positive energy, encouragement, and belief. This makes each person better, and it makes the team better. Ways we can put this into practice are to believe in great outcomes and in each other. We can also trust that our challenges are opportunities to help us learn and grow and make us stronger and better."

"Our beliefs are demonstrated by what we say and do. We must make sure our beliefs align with our vision and goals. If we have big goals, we have to believe big. If we want to accomplish something great as a team, we have to believe it's possible. If we believe it is possible, we will work hard to achieve it."

"That was great John and Dan, thank you!" said Coach David. "We are going to write some belief statements this week on the board and practice saying them until they become a part of our beliefs and actions as a team. Okay, Markell, you're up for tomorrow with James, and your word is Ownership."

Chapter Four

Ownership

The next day, Markell entered the locker room first, carrying a notebook with scribbled notes filling the first few pages. He wore a serious look as he walked in and declared, "Coach, I OWNED this assignment. I owned it!" Then he gave him a big smile. "Get it?"

The players leaned up against their lockers as Markell shared the word he and James had explored. "Our word is Ownership."

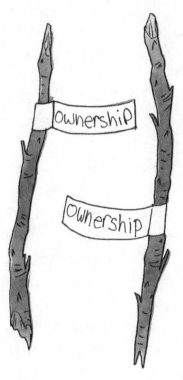

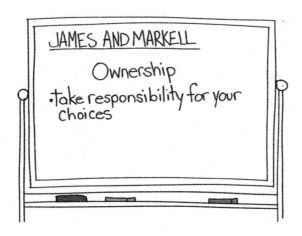

"We thought about this a lot and we think ownership is about taking responsibility for your words and actions. Like if you make a mistake or a bad choice, you can't pass it onto someone else because you did it, not them. And even if someone else made a mistake or contributed to a loss or failure, you must see your part in it. Don't blame them. Look at yourself and realize your choices are your own, and if you can see that then you can make new choices that are better for yourself and also for your team."

"I make a lot of excuses. I didn't really think about it until I sat down last night to do this word with James and I realized that I blame everyone and everything but me. I think the truth is that deep down, I blame myself so much for things that I have to spread it to others because it's hard to always feel like you're messing up, and easier to pretend it's someone else's fault. But I realized that when we own up to something, it's easier to let it go, because now we can fix it and make a new choice."

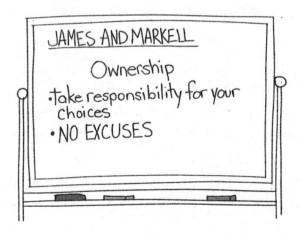

JAMES AND MARKELL

Ownership
- take responsibility for your choices
- NO EXCUSES

"I still feel like I failed the team last year because I should have passed the ball off on that last play. I took a shot that I had no business taking and we lost our chance to tie it up. That's been eating at me for a long time. I'm going to start by owning that one right now."

The locker room was quiet. Then Shawn spoke up. "Markell, you've made that shot before. There was no reason for you to think you couldn't make it when you took it. We had a lot of opportunities to get baskets and we just missed. We had a lot of rebounds that should have been ours, but we didn't get them. We all missed that shot with you."

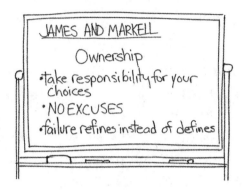

JAMES AND MARKELL

Ownership
- take responsibility for your choices
- NO EXCUSES
- failure refines instead of defines

Coach David smiled. "That's ownership, guys. That, right there, is exactly it. Our mistakes and failures don't define us. They refine us and make us better. I'm proud of you! Let's get our belief statements up on the board and then head out to practice. Moose! You're up tomorrow. What's your word?"

Moose, who was named after his spirit animal for his big plays and unbelievable vertical jump, looked at his stick and replied, "Connection, Coach, and I'm with Greg."

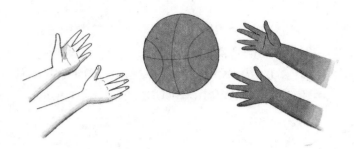

Markell felt relieved after admitting how he felt about that shot from last season. He wrote his belief statement on the board to back up his admission to the team. It said, "I can pass the ball to someone in a better position to score because I trust my teammates to take care of the ball."

But as they were leaving the locker room, he looked back at all those sticks in the lockers and knew they weren't any closer to figuring out how to keep the sticks from breaking. He really wanted to wear that new uniform. His uniform from last season was definitely getting too small.

Chapter Five

Connection

The next day as the team sat in the locker room, Ant, the team's point guard, approached Coach David. "Hey Coach, I got it," he declared. "Check out my practice stick and see if you can break it!"

Coach David held up the stick and examined it. It was soaked end to end in some sort of glue and wrapped with string. He laughed and said, "Well, this was creative. Did you ruin the kitchen table to get the stick to look like this?"

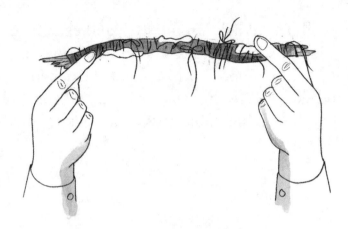

Ant rubbed the back of his neck. "Yeah," he admitted, "my mom wasn't too happy about my art project."

Coach lifted the stick between his finger and thumb on each hand and the players made a drum roll sound.

SNAP! The stick snapped in half, glue
and all.

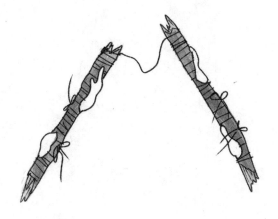

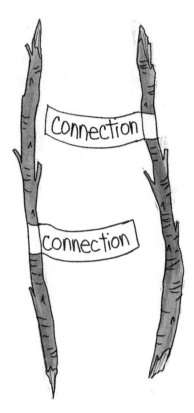

The guys let out a moan and grumbled as
Moose and Greg headed to the front of the
group to present their word. "Okay guys,"
Moose began, "our word is Connection."

"When a team is connected, they feel more committed to each other. It's a team's connection that leads to commitment. I found a good article about that. We make connections by sharing who we are, talking about our struggles and challenges, making time to have hard or meaningful conversations, and listening to each other."

"We both felt connected with Markell yesterday when he talked about taking ownership because we have felt that way too. It also showed us that Markell is worried about his performance even though sometimes it comes across that he only focuses on others' mistakes." Moose looked at Markell. "Sorry man, just sometimes you come off that way."

"Anyway, being connected off the court means we will play more connected on the court. Ways we can apply this are to have more opportunities to get to know each other, to be honest with each other, and to build more trust between us."

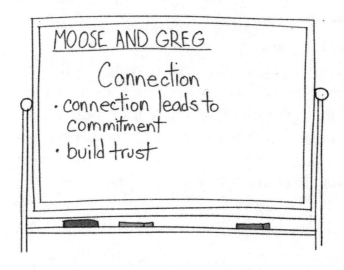

MOOSE AND GREG

Connection
- connection leads to commitment
- build trust

"Moose and Greg, great job, guys! Thanks!" said Coach. "We are going to start right now forming connections by sharing a defining moment in each of our lives. I want each of you to tell us about an event or moment in your life that really shaped who you are as a person. Everything shared in this room must stay here inside our team circle."

Coach went first. He shared how last year became a defining moment for him because he knew he needed to be a better coach. He told them how much talent they had and that it was his job to get them to become a better team. He failed, and yet it made him want to be better and approach this season differently.

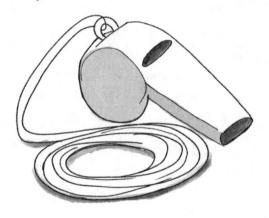

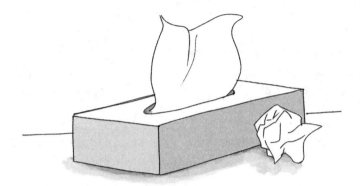

The returning players had tears in their eyes as Coach shared from his heart. All throughout the off-season they had felt like they had let him down by losing in the first round, but now they realized Coach didn't blame them. He blamed himself and it made them want to play even harder for him.

Then each player shared their own defining moment, and they learned things about each other they had no idea had happened. Many of the guys felt a wave of emotions as they shared their stories. Some even cried. The walls of pride and ego came crumbling down and their vulnerability paved the way for meaningful relationships, stronger connections, and a greater commitment to each other.

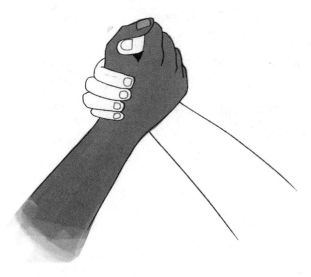

The team building took longer than expected, which left only 20 minutes for practice. But Coach David knew the defining moment exercise was well worth it and would have a much greater impact on the team than more time spent on shooting and passing drills.

At the end of practice Coach David announced, "Tomorrow we'll explore two words. Deshaun is up first. What's your word, Deshaun?"

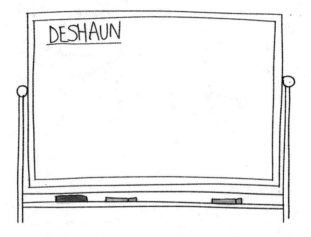

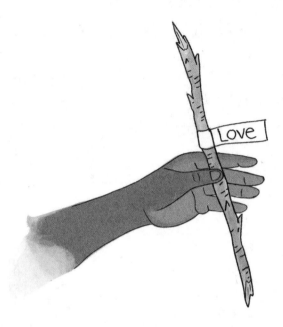

Deshaun gently lifted his stick and read his word out loud, sounding slightly embarrassed. "Love, and I'm partnered with Isaiah."

"Okay, and Thomas, you're going too. What's your word?"

Thomas shouted out, "Inclusion, Coach, and I'm partnered with Rennie!"

DESHAUN AND ISAIAH
Love

THOMAS AND RENNIE
Inclusion

Chapter Six

Love

The next afternoon, Deshaun and Isaiah went first, sharing their word as the guys gathered in the locker room once again before practice.

Isaiah was too nervous to talk so Deshaun led the way and began talking about love.

"We found some articles on love and leadership that were actually pretty interesting. Leaders who show their teams they love them and care about them have more committed players. A team that loves each other is able to challenge each other to work harder and sacrifice more."

"A team with a lot of love doesn't need a lot of rules."

"Love creates trust, trust leads to commitment, and commitment leads to sacrifice. If you love your team, you will give your all to the team. Love also makes people more accountable. If you love your team, you will want to be your best for them, and you want to help them be great too. We found a tweet that said, 'A team with a lot of love doesn't need a lot of rules.'"

"Love will drive a team to be great for each other. Love also helps with having more patience, understanding, and a desire to succeed together. So, uh, we should probably find a way to love our teammates even when they do stupid stuff like putting all your underwear in the ice bath . . . Shawn!"

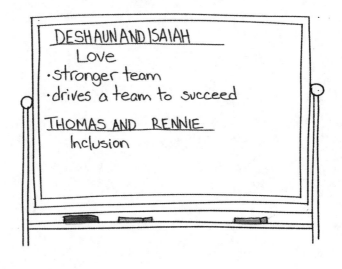

DESHAUN AND ISAIAH
  Love
· stronger team
· drives a team to succeed

THOMAS AND RENNIE
  Inclusion

The team laughed at the prank from last season, but not as loud as Shawn, who still remembered Deshaun finding all his underwear floating in frigid ice water when it was time to dress for a big game.

Chapter Seven

Inclusion

Thomas spoke next, and as one of the biggest contributors on the team, this was the perfect word for him to share. "Okay, so our word is Inclusion."

"Inclusion is important for each player to feel like they are a part of the team. A big part of inclusion is the good feeling you get when you contribute to the team and are recognized and valued for who you are and the contribution you've made. When you feel like you are helping to build the future of the team, you feel more connected to the team and the team's outcomes."

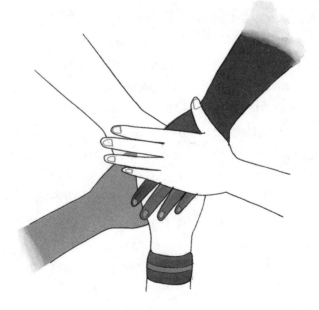

"Rennie and I talked about it, and to put this into practice we need to show up and contribute something of value to the team no matter how we're feeling that day. But we also need to make sure our teammates feel that their contributions are valued by demonstrating appreciation and gratitude. When our teammates are feeling down, we need to encourage them and highlight how their contributions matter. Then they will feel inspired to continue to give of themselves to the greater good of the team."

"I really like this word because sometimes when I've felt worthless because of how bad I played, I've had a teammate tell me how I did something that helped them and the team, and that made me feel like I belonged. So thanks, guys, for picking me up when I needed it and thanks to Rennie for helping me see how this applies to society as well."

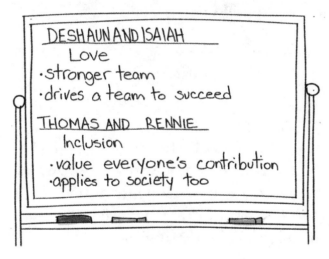

DESHAUN AND ISAIAH
Love
• stronger team
• drives a team to succeed

THOMAS AND RENNIE
Inclusion
• value everyone's contribution
• applies to society too

"We need to include those who don't feel like they're included. We need to recognize and value everyone for their contributions to our community and society. Inclusion helps us build a stronger team at every level."

Coach David was impressed. The players' efforts to learn and share their words far exceeded his expectations. He could see that they were growing with each word. He raised the stick he had in his hand into the air.

"Okay, great stuff, guys! Only one more night until our first game of the season and the chance to wear those new uniforms! You're doing a great job on the words, but the other part of the challenge is going to be tough. I believe you can solve this problem, though. Don't give up. Prove you have what it takes to meet the challenge! Let's go hit the court."

"Tomorrow's words are Consistency and Hope. I'm going to be doing those for you so that you can focus on solving the stick challenge."

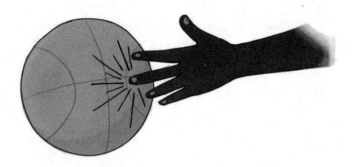

The guys headed to the court to practice for the season opener. About an hour into practice, during some passing and shooting drills, Markell reached for a pass and he heard a loud POP, followed by an intense pain shooting through his hand.

"Ahhhh!" he yelled as he grabbed his hand and bent down, trying to quiet the pain. "I jammed it. Oh man, I jammed it really good." His knuckle was already turning purple and swelling up.

Coach David took a look at his hand puffing up and sent him to grab a bag of ice and told him to take it easy and see Julie, the school nurse, first thing tomorrow. He wasn't going to get any more quality practice in after that and he was better off resting it until the swelling went down. It was usually the first day of practice that somebody jammed a finger. He was surprised they had made it this long. The drills the first week are fast and intense, and fingers are always in the way.

Chapter Eight

Consistency and Hope

The next day at practice Markell showed up with his hand badly swollen and bruised. He told Coach David that he hadn't had time to get to the nurse yet, so David called his wife, the school athletic trainer, and asked her to come by. She was still in her office and promised to come down to the locker room to look at Markell's hand and tape it up.

Coach David stood in front of his team. Knowing they hadn't solved the stick mystery, they were gazing mournfully at the box of new uniforms with a look of defeat on their faces.

"The last two words are Consistency and Hope. I'll start with consistency. We can't bring our best effort one day and a weak effort another day. We can't let emotions, fears, or doubts affect the amount of effort that we give to each other and to our team. To build a great team we must be consistent with our effort each and every day."

"Consistency is what creates excellence because we are what we repeatedly do, not what we say we'll do or want to do. We must be consistent with our attitude, effort, leadership, teamwork, habits, and our pursuit of greatness. When we are consistent, we'll see that our outcome is determined by our commitment to the process along the way. It means that our actions are based on our commitments rather than being controlled by emotion or events."

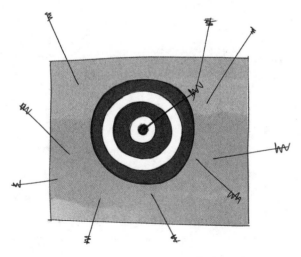

"In addition to being consistent, we must also always remain hopeful. No matter the circumstance, we must always maintain hope that our love, beliefs, connections, inclusiveness, contributions, and consistency will get us where we need to be. I can see in your faces that you've lost hope in your chance to take the court in those awesome new uniforms, but your time is not up!"

"When you lose hope, you can't win a game or the future. You can't move forward. You get stuck. You focus on where you are instead of where you want to be. So keep hope alive. Keep fighting, because it's not over until it's over. Do you understand?"

COACH DAVID
Consistency
- consistent effort every day
- consistency = excellence

Hope
- always remain hopeful
- hope → future

Chapter Nine

Unbreakable

As Coach David was talking, his wife, Amy, arrived in the locker room. She visited with Markell in the back corner of the room, explained that his finger didn't appear to be broken but was definitely sprained and might need an X-ray if it didn't feel better in a few days. She began to tape his injured finger to the finger beside it, telling him that the injured finger would be stronger if it was taped to another finger next to it for support. She reached behind her to grab more tape and when she turned around Markell had run across the locker room to his teammates.

"Give me your sticks!" he shouted frantically. "Everybody, give me your sticks!"

The players all tentatively handed over their sticks to Markell, wondering what was going on.

"Shawn, give me your shoelaces!" said Markell.

"What? You can't have my shoelaces. I need those!"

Markell looked him in the eyes. "Do you trust me or not? Give me your shoelaces!"

Shawn reached down and pulled out his laces. Markell laid the laces down on the floor and stacked the sticks together into a bundle. He tied the laces tightly around the bundle at each end and then handed the bundle to Coach David.

"Break it!" he shouted.

David smiled as he held up the bundle and tried to bend it in two. It didn't budge. He then thrust the bundle down across his knee trying to snap the twigs in half, but nothing happened. It was too strong.

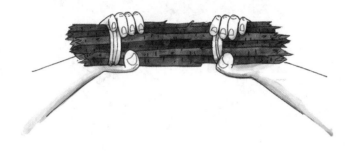

The locker room erupted in cheers and chants as the players realized they had met the challenge. Markell shouted over the noise, "I'll take a large 'please and thank you'!"

Shawn looked up at Coach David. "Coach," he said, "we had all the pieces to win. We just weren't in it together."

Chapter Ten

Stick Together

Coach David nodded. He saw the positive shift in his team as they grasped what can happen when people stick together. They realized in that moment that together they truly were unstoppable. They weren't strong enough on their own, but they would be stronger together when life and the competition tried to break them.

"Guys, any team can be a group of sticks. But team members need each other to be strong. Only a team who believes, loves, includes everyone, is consistent, takes ownership, connects, and has hope all bundled together can come out on top and reach their true potential. We can't ever forget that!" said Coach David as the team gathered in a circle with their arms around each other.

"That's what team means; it's a group that sticks together through adversity to pursue a shared vision and purpose, and seeks to accomplish something great together. We can't ever be whole until we are bound together. As a united team we cannot and will not be broken ever again. Last season we broke under pressure. This year we can do it better. We will stick together and do it together."

Coach David led that team out onto the court that night for practice. For the rest of the season, they played and fought for each other. They played to pursue greatness together, and they charged through the playoffs to win the championship.

The players all wrote, "Stick together for greatness," on their shoes and wrote the word they had shared on their practice basketball.

After the season and for years to come, that bundle of sticks with the words on them, tied together by Shawn's shoelaces, hung in the locker room as a reminder that a team that sticks together becomes stronger together.

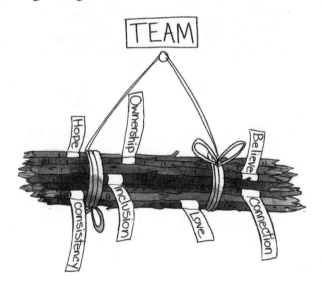

Every year the seniors would teach the new players the "Story of the Sticks" and demonstrate the weakness of one stick versus the strength of a bundle of sticks bound together. The team would then get their new uniforms and experience the positive impact and the results of sticking together.

It would be a lesson they would carry with them for the rest of their lives, and into their future careers. Rather than falling short as a group of individuals, they understood the power of becoming a real team.

Resources to Stick Together

If you are interested in a keynote or team workshop based on *Stick Together*, visit StickTogetherBook.com. Email info@ JonGordon.com. Call 904-285-6842.

Visit StickTogetherBook.com for:

- An action plan
- Posters
- Videos
- Resources to help your team stick together
- Bulk book orders

About the Authors

JON GORDON has inspired millions of readers around the world. He is the author of 24 books, including ten bestsellers: *The Energy Bus*, *The Carpenter*, *Training Camp*, *You Win in the Locker Room First*, *The Power of Positive Leadership*, *The Power of a Positive Team*, *The Coffee Bean*, *Stay Positive*, *The Garden*, and *Relationship Grit*. He is passionate about developing positive leaders, organizations, and teams.

KATE LEAVELL is a speaker, workshop facilitator, and author of *Confessions of an Imperfect Coach*. She is a former NCAA coach, corporate sales consultant, and Coaches Education Trainer and now works with teams and leaders across the country to boost performance, connection, and energy. She is passionate about teaching strategies that turn a powerful vision into reality, while unifying teammates around their purpose and mission.

About the Illustrator

KATIE MAZEIKA is an illustrator and digital artist who primarily works in Photoshop. She lives in Northeast Ohio with her husband and two kids.

www.katiemazeika.com

Other Books by Jon Gordon

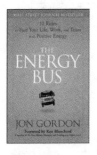

The Energy Bus

A man whose life and career are in shambles learns from a unique bus driver and set of passengers how to overcome adversity. Enjoy an enlightening ride of positive energy that is improving the way leaders lead, employees work, and teams function.

www.TheEnergyBus.com

The No Complaining Rule

Follow a VP of Human Resources who must save herself and her company from ruin and discover proven principles and an actionable plan to win the battle against individual and organizational negativity.

www.NoComplainingRule.com

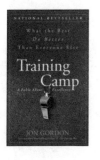

Training Camp

This inspirational story about a small guy with a big heart, and a special coach who guides him on a quest for excellence, reveals the 11 winning habits that separate the best individuals and teams from the rest.

www.TrainingCamp11.com

The Shark and the Goldfish

Delightfully illustrated, this quick read is packed with tips and strategies on how to respond to challenges beyond your control in order to thrive during waves of change.

www.SharkandGoldfish.com

Soup

The newly appointed CEO of a popular soup company is brought in to reinvigorate the brand and bring success back to a company that has fallen on hard times. Through her journey, discover the key ingredients to unite, engage, and inspire teams to create a culture of greatness.

www.Soup11.com

The Seed

Go on a quest for the meaning and passion behind work with Josh, an up-and-comer at his company who is disenchanted with his job. Through Josh's cross-country journey, you'll find surprising new sources of wisdom and inspiration in your own business and life.

www.Seed11.com

One Word

One Word is a simple concept that delivers powerful life change! This quick read will inspire you to simplify your life and work by focusing on just one word for this year. *One Word* creates clarity, power, passion, and life-change. When you find your word, live it, and share it, your life will become more rewarding and exciting than ever.

www.getoneword.com

The Positive Dog

We all have two dogs inside of us. One dog is positive, happy, optimistic, and hopeful. The other dog is negative, mad, pessimistic, and fearful. These two dogs often fight inside us, but guess who wins? The one you feed the most. *The Positive Dog* is an inspiring story that not only reveals the strategies and benefits of being positive, but also an essential truth: being positive doesn't just make you better; it makes everyone around you better.

www.feedthepositivedog.com

The Carpenter

The Carpenter is Jon Gordon's most inspiring book yet—filled with powerful lessons and success strategies. Michael wakes up in the hospital with a bandage on his head and fear in his heart after collapsing during a morning jog. When Michael finds out the man who saved his life is a carpenter, he visits him and quickly learns that he is more than just a carpenter; he is also a builder of lives, careers, people, and teams. In this journey, you will learn timeless principles to help you stand out, excel, and make an impact on people and the world.

www.carpenter11.com

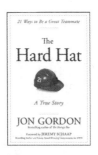

The Hard Hat

A true story about Cornell lacrosse player George Boiardi, *The Hard Hat* is an unforgettable book about a selfless, loyal, joyful, hard-working, competitive, and compassionate leader and teammate, the impact he had on his team and program, and the lessons we can learn from him. This inspirational story will teach you how to build a great team and be the best teammate you can be.

www.hardhat21.com

You Win in the Locker Room First

Based on the extraordinary experiences of NFL Coach Mike Smith and leadership expert Jon Gordon, *You Win in the Locker Room First* offers a rare behind-the-scenes look at one of the most pressure-packed leadership jobs on the planet, and what leaders can learn from these experiences in order to build their own winning teams.

www.wininthelockerroom.com

Life Word

Life Word reveals a simple, powerful tool to help you identify the word that will inspire you to live your best life while leaving your greatest legacy. In the process, you'll discover your why, which will help show you how to live with a renewed sense of power, purpose, and passion.

www.getoneword.com/lifeword

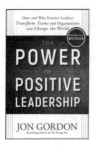

The Power of Positive Leadership

The Power of Positive Leadership is your personal coach for becoming the leader your people deserve. Jon Gordon gathers insights from his bestselling fables to bring you the definitive guide to positive leadership. Difficult times call for leaders who are up to the challenge. Results are the by-product of your culture, teamwork, vision, talent, innovation, execution, and commitment. This book shows you how to bring it all together to become a powerfully positive leader.

www.powerofpositiveleadership.com

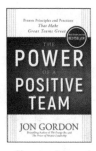

The Power of a Positive Team

In *The Power of a Positive Team*, Jon Gordon draws upon his unique team-building experience, as well as conversations with some of the greatest teams in history, to provide an essential framework of proven practices to empower teams to work together more effectively and achieve superior results.

www.PowerOfAPositiveTeam.com

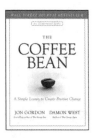

The Coffee Bean

From bestselling author Jon Gordon and rising star Damon West comes *The Coffee Bean*: an illustrated fable that teaches readers how to transform their environment, overcome challenges, and create positive change.

www.coffeebeanbook.com

Stay Positive

Fuel yourself and others with positive energy—inspirational quotes and encouraging messages to live by from bestselling author, Jon Gordon. Keep this little book by your side, read from it each day, and feed your mind, body, and soul with the power of positivity.

www.StayPositiveBook.com

The Garden

The Garden is an enlightening and encouraging fable that helps readers overcome The 5 D's (doubt, distortion, discouragement, distractions, and division) in order to find more peace, focus, connection, and happiness. Jon tells a story of teenage twins, who through the help of a neighbor and his special garden, find ancient wisdom, life-changing lessons, and practical strategies to overcome the fear, anxiety, and stress in their lives.

www.readthegarden.com

Relationship Grit

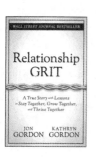

Bestselling author Jon Gordon is back with another life-affirming book. This time, he teams up with Kathryn Gordon, his wife of 23 years, for a look at what it takes to build strong relationships. In *Relationship Grit*, the Gordons reveal what brought them together, what kept them together through difficult times, and what continues to sustain their love and passion for one another to this day.

www.relationshipgritbook.com

The Energy Bus for Kids

The illustrated children's adaptation of the bestselling book *The Energy Bus* tells the story of George, who, with the help of his school bus driver, Joy, learns that if he believes in himself, he'll find the strength to overcome any challenge. His journey teaches kids how to overcome negativity, bullies, and everyday challenges to be their best.
www.EnergyBusKids.com

Thank You and Good Night

Thank You and Good Night is a beautifully illustrated book that shares the heart of gratitude. Jon Gordon takes a little boy and girl on a fun-filled journey from one perfect moonlit night to the next. During their adventurous days and nights, the children explore the people, places, and things they are thankful for.

The Hard Hat for Kids

The Hard Hat for Kids is an illustrated guide to teamwork. Adapted from the bestseller *The Hard Hat*, this uplifting story presents practical insights and life-changing lessons that are immediately applicable to everyday situations, giving kids—and adults—a new outlook on cooperation, friendship, and the selfless nature of true teamwork.

www.HardHatforKids.com

One Word for Kids

If you could choose only one word to help you have your best year ever, what would it be? *Love? Fun? Believe? Brave?* It's probably different for each person. How you find your word is just as important as the word itself. And once you know your word, what do you do with it? In *One Word for Kids,* bestselling author Jon Gordon—along with coauthors Dan Britton and Jimmy Page—asks these questions to children and adults of all ages, teaching an important life lesson in the process.

www.getoneword.com/kids

The Coffee Bean for Kids

From the bestselling authors of *The Coffee Bean*, inspire and encourage children with this transformative tale of personal strength. Perfect for parents, teachers, and children who wish to overcome negativity and challenging situations, *The Coffee Bean for Kids* teaches readers about the potential that each one of us has to lead, influence, and make a positive impact on others and the world.

www.coffeebeankidsbook.com